# One Last Chance

## A POEM

## Una Ultima Oportunidad

Spanish Translation by Maria E. Gomez

Illustrated by Jose Luis Diaz

## Sonia Gomez-Neri

Mary's Press
San Diego, California

Mary's Press
San Diego, California

All rights reserved. No part of this book may be reproduced or transmitted in any form or by any means, electronic or mechanical, including photocopying, recording or by any information storage and retrieval system, without written permission from the author, except for the inclusion of brief quotations in a review.

Copyright © 2009

ISBN 13: 978-0-615-17628-4

## Dedications

I would like to dedicate this first edition to the people who mean the most to me:

Roman, Sofia, Isabella, RJ, and Raul – the loves of my life, Maria, my mom, mentor, and translator, Laura, Ramsey, and Papi, Maggie, to whom this poem was written for,

And to my heavenly mother who has inspired me to write my soul's passion and to seek a life of virtue with every meditation.

Truly, truly I say to you, he who hears my word and believes him who sent me, has eternal life; he does not come into judgment, but has passed from death to life.

John 5:24

# One Last Chance

## Una Ultima Oportunidad

One last hug

One last kiss

One last chance

Is all I wish

Un último abrazo

Un último beso

Una última oportunidad

Es por loque rezo

To hear I love you

One last time

From your lips

A love divine

Pa' oir te amo

Una última vez

Un amor divino

De tus labios me dés

One last comfort

Of your embrace

One last chance

To touch your face

Un último consuelo

De tu abrazo sentir

Una última oportunidad

Pa' ver tu rostro sonreír

One last laugh

One last tear

I'll hold the memory

Of them dear

Una última lágrima

Una última caricia

En mi mente vivirá

Esta memoria tan bellísima

One last word

Of your advice

To teach me how

To live my life

Una última palabra

De tu consejo oir

Que me enseñes como debo

Mi vida vivir

One last moment

For us to share

A special moment

To show we care

Un último momento

Pa' nosotros compartir

Un momento especial

Nuestro cariño revivir

One last chance

Before you leave

To say good-bye

And not to grieve

Una última oportunidad

Antes de partir

Para decirnos adios

Y este dolor no sentir

To remember instead

With hope and love

That we'll meet again

In heaven above

En cambio recordar

Con esperanza y gran amor

Que nos vamos a encontrar

En un lugar mejor

Until that day

When it's my time

With my last breath

Your name I'll cry

Hasta ese día

Cuando mi hora esté por llegar

Con mi último suspiro

Tu nombre voy a llamar

And on that day

The last will end

For that is when

Forever begins …

Y cuando llegue ese día

Lo último se terminará

Porque eso es cuando

La eternidad empezará

## About the Poem

This poem was inspired from the passing of a dear loved one, Maggie Esparza. She left our world unexpectedly and she will always be remembered as a woman with a kind heart and loving nature.

There are so many times we long to have *one last chance* with a loved one who has passed on. If I were to have one last chance with my dad I would want him to know my children and spend time with them. I would want him to find peace before he left. Most of all, I would want him to know I loved him and I appreciated the time I had with him. I am the person I am today, thanks, in part, to the impression he left upon my soul. Although I still miss him beyond words I believe he has found peace and happiness with our Lord. I know one day, when my time has come, he will be there to greet me and welcome me home.

## Acknowledgments

With deepest appreciation to Jose Luis Diaz whose beautiful drawings are everything I envisioned and more.

To Veronica Williams for helping me with the design and layout of the book.

To Natalie German for her assistance with the front cover.

To my sister Laura and my cousin Janie for lending me their hands.

To Monica, Janie and Hita for helping to edit the Spanish translation.

To Jared and Madge for reviving my dream to publish my poem and providing me the guidance to accomplish this through STRATEGIES.

To my mother for staying true to the heart and rhythm of the poem in her Spanish translation, for driving me here and there without much complaint, and for praying with me every day.

www.ingramcontent.com/pod-product-compliance
Lightning Source LLC
Chambersburg PA
CBHW071418290426
44108CB00014B/1873